Acknowledgement

First of all I want to thank my family
for motivating me to become an
author and for fulfilling my dream
project

I want to special thank my elder
brother arif for showing me the way
to read and understand the different
life hacks which are discussed in this
book

I also want to thank the entrepreneur,
author and influencer mr.stefen who
is owner of project life mastery brand
his YouTube videos are so inspiring
which made me to write this book and
publish it.

Indeed the philosophy of warren buffet, Charlie munger, Robert kiyosaki and other great investor who made their great wealth from scratch. Inspired me to gain the financial knowledge obviously a special thanks to those all of them.

Introduction

As we all know that money doesn't solve your all problems it can solve the problems which are associated to wealth but to be honest one must be know that our maximum problems are associated to wealth like paying our monthly rents, bills, tax's etc.

This book is designed to throw a light on the matters of money and how one can manage wealth smartly to be financially free.

There are 3.8 billion population across the globe which is middle class which makes 48% of whole population this is because illiteracy in financial management .I'm not *saying that being in middle or the low class is bad but not knowing the reason why you are in that class is too bad so it's necessary to get awareness in the people to know financial management and to learn to grow their money to be financially free.*

In this book you will learn how to make money from scratch I mean with low money .if you have even 10 bucks this book teaches you how to manage that 10 bucks even it is very low but it can make a lot .the person who know the power of money don't look it as low money or useless money I.e. looking this bucks to buy snakes or just not considering it as money.

If you ask me what is the one thing which you will suggest from this book so I will recommend you to read process of passive income through real estate investment and i highly recommend all the reader to implement that to supplement your income.

Contents

Introduction

Chapter 1.

Why your little money won't solve your problems

Reading to the name of chapter one can say that my money solves my all problems such as paying my monthly bills, eating out with friends etc.

But I'm speaking of little money i.e. insufficient money after paying of all the bills and payments best of all concept in the world of financial

management is *"pay yourself first"*
what it actually means?

It means saving money first. I know it
sounds weird but this habit can make
you financially free.

Power of money

There is nothing like little money or
extra money it's all about the
mentality which a person has from
their surroundings and childhood I'm
not saying that if you are poor or
mediocre your upbringings are worse.
I just want you to let you know that
financial wisdom is at most important
to leave stress free life.

For example if I gave 3.1 crores to a
middle class young boy what he will
do?

Most probably he will buy a Lamborghini new luxurious car to show off his friends and neighbors and he dress himself as superrich despite of being in middle class he don't realize to make more money with that he just want to look rich . Considering the same amount of money given to boy who actually wants to become rich guess what he will do?

There are two possibilities that this guy can do

1. He will consult to an expert advice who know how to make investments

2. He can just do his own research to make more money with that

Normally speaking if he follows both the points he can reach his financial goals early.

This is the mentality which differentiate super rich from a middle class and poor .continuing the above 2nd example to know the opportunities with that 3.1 crores.

He can do investments with that money so that "money works for him instead of working for money"

The number one investment with low risk is and long term return is real estate I'm not suggesting you to invest whole amount in one property based on locations prices may vary but with this amount you can buy multiple properties but how?

There is procedure for this which we will discuss in upcoming chapter "significance of investment" if you learn that procedure and implement it I guarantee you no one besides god can stop you to be financially free and enjoy your life in long term. But the above example was regarding a huge amount of money i.e. 3.1 crores

Speaking about middle class and giving example with huge amount can sound ridiculous but I used that example to just differentiate the thoughts

Of actually being rich and trying to look rich.

But to start your journey to become financially free you need to sacrifice some things initially so that you can enjoy your future when everyone is doing 9-5 jobs

Again comes the concept of paying yourself first before paying your bills

This concept you can see in all most every financial book everyone reads this but only few follow because to say, read and listen it's easy but those who are actually willing to become financially free they the legends who implement it and succeed in life.

I request the readers don't just read and leave implement it.

Concept of pay yourself first

The concept is very simple fix the percentage which you want to save every month it should not be less than 10% it must be more than that it can be 90% if you can manage. But fixing minimum of 10% is most important.

After deciding that keep that percentage of money aside every month if you are employee or else for every income.

Then comes the necessary expenses such as your rent, bills, food etc. pay it now.

Now the money which is remaining you do whatever you want you can go for outings with friends or you

can do the shopping but remember
that this comes last after saving
your money of decided percentage
and paying necessary expenses.
The money which you have saved let
it become huge amount may be
500% of your income then you can
invest it so that you can earn passive
income
(Which means income generated
when you sleep in other words
money work for you).
There are lots of investing domains
through which you can make passive
income which we will discuss in next
chapter.

"one year of dedication and

> *hard work can move you*
>
> *fifteen years ahead"*

Chapter 2.

Significance and opportunities of Investing

As we have seen in chapter one the thinking makes one to be rich or poor and not to look at opportunities.

This chapter mainly focuses on how your money can grow by investing. But before going to learn the investment process we need to know why it is necessary to learn investing is it really that much important to know. If we ignore it can't we become financially free? What if we just save money only for long term can't we become rich? All this type of question arises in mind when we listen about investing and one more thing people who are in 50s and 60s they think that it's not there cup of tea because they are already old and they can't plan long term now so they ignore it and just survive with their savings but to be honest this is the age of wisdom and knowledge because they have learn so many things in their 20s 30s and 40s it's the time of implementation and mentoring others instead they think that they are old and they can't do anything now this is the myth which everyone must avoid to be happy especially for non-techy uncles.

Now let's get back to the topic and find the answers of the above questions

Inflation

Before learning investing one must learn what is inflation we all know that this term is widely used by accountants and persons who belongs to economics background by thinking this we just ignore this terms but this terms plays an important role in everyone's life whether he/she belongs to any country.

In simple words inflation means a general increase in prices and fall in the purchasing value of money.

This means as the year's passes we lose the value of our money. Have you heard your parents or elders who are double to your age saying that "we used to so and so thing at very cheap price now look how expensive this things are"

This is fact that our currencies or money loosing it's valve even if we save our money we won't be able to get exact returns which we have now . So to be at safe side one must invest so that the value of money get increase year after year or based on the domain which we select.

According to defination we know that we loose the value of money due to inflation but how much value this the question arises.remember that history repeats over and over again so to speculate the future we must look at the past how we gain or loose the graphs helps you to understand clear.

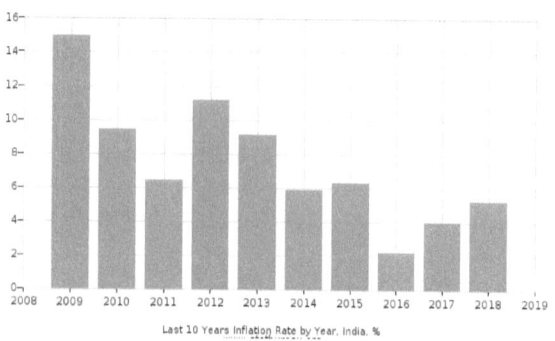

Last 10 Years Inflation Rate by Year, India, %

The graphs gives us inflation rates of a country India this is just for example it can be any other country you can look at your economy just google search the inflation rate and type the name of your country in which you live you will come to know that how much money you are losing every year by just saving.

By considering the above example we can see that the average inflation rate of country is 7% approx. to speculate the future inflation it may be 4+or- 2

It may be 6 or it may be 2 depending on countries growth.

Well this is all about inflation now if we save 100 rupees now at your home then in the next year that 100 will be 94 or 98 in value based on inflation so if the banks are providing interest of 6% there is no increase in your value of money it remains same but it looks like you have gain some additional money so making FD and saving in banks is worthless.

Remember the concept of pay yourself first in that we have discussed to save money first. If you consider inflation in that then you won't be able to invest because you won't have money now .we are saving that money to invest not to keep it for long term.

Now with this we can conclude that saving is also risky.

One of the well-known investor warren buffet said that "if you don't find a way to make money while you sleep you will work until you die"

In order to be free from inflation and gain financial freedom we must find a way to make money while sleeping i.e. passive income without this soon or later anyone can have financial problem.

Investing opportunities

I have divided investment opportunities into 3 categories

1. Low investment high return

2. Medium investment medium return

3. High investment ultra-high return

Low investment

Before starting investment one must learn process of investing no doubt

*that without practical knowledge
there are more possibilities of
failure but we can reduce these
failure possibilities by gaining
theoretical knowledge
If I say you that you can invest your
little amount of money with zero risk
and high return so you will be
curious to know that it's the
investment you have been already
doing that is educating yourself
Getting financial knowledge through
books and courses is the best ever
investment you can do on yourself
.these investments never despair you
Because this knowledge you can
implement in your daily life.*

Instead of paying recharges of Netflix to watch TV series you can invest that money on yourself by purchasing books which offers you financial knowledge which in turn can change your life like you have did this time.

Next comes the courses.my advise to each and every reader of this book is to select the course which will offer you great wealth in future for example real estate courses, digital marketing ,stock market courses etc. you can select any course based on your passion and interest

After selecting the course educate yourself on that topic say real estate it's the best investment you can have

you may select any other.

<u>The process of educating yourself</u>

<u>after selecting a course</u>

1. Selecting course which you desire

2. Educating yourself on that topic

through books

3. Select the best channels from

YouTube based on that topic and

watch at least

One video a day remember that

you must select multiple channels

who

Really implemented it.

4. Watch the videos and make notes

daily if required if can remember for

long run than its ok you can just

watch and save the tricks and tactics in your brain

5. By doing all these don't forget to save some part of money monthly because at the end you need to implement it through capital

6. After some time when you are sure of particular stream you can do investments in that particular domain

If you follow above 6 steps you will be financially free may be in less than 5 years because technology is growing rapidly you can utilize multiple sources in a day which was not possible in ancient times.

At the end of this topic I will say that the best investment you must *make is to invest on yourself by educating yourself in specialized skill*

Medium investment medium returns

When I say medium return then it means medium risk involve in this investment.

These are very common in middle class I won't explain these in-depth because now a days everyone know this.

They are as follows

1. Bank FD

2. Mutual funds

3. Index funds and elf's

4. Chit funds

All these investment are very
common because they offer medium
risk and constant medium return
however I will try to just throw the
light on all of these.

Usually when we have excess money
most of us save in banks as fd which
shows you 8 or may be 9% of return
by seeing this most of us mesmerized
by this but the reality is even if you
get 9% return as interest per annum
you actually gain 3-4% which is
very less return by considering the
inflation of 5-6% as discussed
earlier in this chapter.so why to
invest in that fds instead we can do
our own investments by just little

effort and gaining specialized knowledge.

Next comes index funds, mutual funds and chit funds all these funds will also offer you medium returns with medium risk.

I am not saying that don't invest in this type of domains. If you are very sensitive to risk and if your risk reward ratio is less then I highly recommend you to invest in this which will give you constant returns Anyways we all know very well about all of these the knowledge about all of these you can get anywhere. Let's move to next.

High investment and ultra -high returns

By saying high investment it doesn't mean that you need large capital to do these investment it means you need lot of courage to do this investment because in these list there are few which have very high risk and obviously large return so be careful while investing in this. They are as follows

1. _Gold_
2. _Silver_
3. _Real estate_
4. _Direct investment in stock market i.e. equity investing_

Investing in Gold

Investing in gold is not like buying stocks or bonds. You can take physical possession of gold by buying either gold coins or gold bullion. Bullion is gold in bar form, with a stamp on it. The stamp contains the purity level and the amount of gold contained in the bar. The value of the bullion or coin comes from its precious metals content and not its rarity and condition, and it can change throughout the day. You can buy bullion or coins from some banks, dealers, brokerage firms, and the U.S. Mint, which has been producing gold coins and bullion for investment since 1986.

You can also buy stock in gold mining companies, gold futures contracts, gold-focused exchange-traded funds (ETFs), and other regular financial instruments. If investors purchase a gold-backed ETF, they are purchasing shares of a trust's ownership in gold, but have no claim to the physical gold itself.

Gold delivers return of over 116% in the last 10 years, 35%in past one year.

In India, gold prices have jumped over 116 percent in the last 10 years, rising from Rs 18,000 per 10 grams in 2010 to Rs 39,000 till date. On a 10-

year basis, the Nifty has returned 135%against gold's 116 percent.

Note-Investing in gold with the idea it never loses value is the wrong approach. Like any investment or financial asset, gold is subject to supply and demand pressures that cause the price to fluctuate.

Returns on silver

Another precious metal, silver, has appreciated by 72.7% during the decade. However, it has delivered negative returns in five out of the last 10 years. During 2013, silver prices fell by 24.3 per cent, its biggest tumble in the decade.

Anyways all the above discussed asserts are non-passive i.e. they *won't generate income monthly or yearly if sell it then you may get high return the next upcoming asserts are most important especially the real estate.*

3. Real estate investment with low money

First get to the fact of returns then we will see how to invest to gain passive income monthly

According to the National Council of Real Estate Investment Fiduciaries (NCREIF), the average 25-year return for private commercial real estate properties held for investment purposes slightly underperformed the S&P 500 Index as of the organization's May 9, 2019, report at 9.4%

Remember the process which I have promised to in chapter 1 that how you can invest in real estate in multiple properties to generate passive income now let's look at that process

<u>Process of investing</u>

1. *As said earlier you need to save some amount of money monthly so that you can get passive income for that. So take out that money now consider it as 3.4 crore as discussed in chapter 1 the person who can own Lamborghini can own a multiple properties.*

2. *After taking that money search for the properties which are getting sold*

on *emi that is* equated monthly installment

3. *now select 10 properties based on your knowledge which you have gained through courses or books*

4. *shortlist those properties to 5*

5. *now finalize any 3 properties and pay the 20% amount of each one for example 90 lakhs each so total would be 2 crore 70 lakhs remaining keep money now*

6. *now check the monthly emi which you have to pay it must be lower than the rent which you can get by renting those properties*

7. *for example the monthly rent which you can get is 20 thousand for each so make the emi for 10 thousand per*

month no matter how long it takes you to pay that emi with interest don't worry your rent will pay your emi every month

8. *as now you are getting 60 thousand rent so pay the emi 30 thousand and remaining 30 is your passive income through which you can fulfill your basic needs*

9. *the emi must be paid through credit card after the payment you just pay the credit card bill with that you can improve your cibil score by paying credit card payments on time if in case you need a loan from bank the bank never checks your ssc memo or college certificate it sees your cibil score and provide you loan so it's*

essential for you to improve the cibil score.

Now you are generating passive income through multiple properties you can gain more selling it after the complete emi payment no doubt the value of the property and rent goes on increasing

Say for example the whole complete payment will be done in 15 years and in those 15 years you have been getting passive income while sleeping now if you don't have home to leave you can take one for livelihood and can sell remaining two with much high price and you can now apply for loan because you have paid consistently the credit card bill your cibil score would be much better to provide loan so bank will offer you loan take it and combine all the money of 2 houses and loan and repeat the process remember that now you have very good amount of wealth compare to last time now you can take more than 5 properties and earn very good passive income

The things which are required for doing all these is courage, patience and some capital which can be obtained by saving consistently that is again comes the concept of pay yourself first

This is best plan for a mediocre man who has very less income with this you can supplement your income

Anyways the above strategy only work if you have accumulated some wealth by saving and your saving must be at least 20% of the property rate.

If your income is so low such that you can't even pay 20% so don't worry there is another plan for this that is stock market investment.

4. Investing in stocks

It is one of the high risk and high return investment but if you follow some principles then you can reduce your risk. As I have said earlier you must educate yourself first.

Before investing in stock market you must read at least more than 15 books on stocks which are recommended by master of investing such as Charlie mugger, warren buffet etc.

After educating yourself now comes the level of confidence and risk reward ratio. You must be confident in selecting stocks and at the same time you must calculate your risk reward ratio that is how much risk you can handle.

The best of all investing in stocks is not growth investing it's value investing that is thinking in other way and not following crowd which is known as contrarian investing many great investor have followed this strategy and accumulated great wealth and some of them are now richest man now according to fobs magazine.

There are two approaches to follow in selecting stocks

1 top down approach

2 bottom up approach

Now just know the meaning of this two you can follow both of them or any one based on your convenience

Top down approach means selecting sector first then selecting best stock in that sector but utilizing details provided to you as ratios and fundamental analysis.

Bottom up approach means selecting stock first and then moving ahead to sector.

In both of the approaches you must check the following

- *Fundamentals of the company*
- *Reputation of company and promoters*
- *Management of the company*
- *Dividend paying record*
- *Technical analysis is not that much necessary for long term investment you can ignore it*
- *Last and most important thing following the philosophy of great investors and not following crowd.*

I again apprise you if you can't tolerate much risk then you should be far away from this investing and if you can handle the stress caused due to loss then the market welcomes you and may reward you with much more returns

"don't be the machine which makes money rather make machine which makes money for you"

Chapter 3

Mindset which is making you a poor guy

When it comes to mindset everyone thinks he is correct and the whole world is doing in a wrong way but the reality is that no one is wrong your mindset allowing you to think in that way

If just accept everyone as right you will be in danger and if you consider everyone is wrong than also you are in threat so what to do now should you listen to others or let it go the answer is simple use your brain Almighty has gifted a great thing to us which is known as brain. The strategies which I have suggested you are just my opinion and my advice to you implementing is up to you if you utter this tricks and tactics to your some of the friends who don't desire to be financially free how much you desire there is more probability that those friends will discourage you for doing that because they don't want to do that so they suggest you too to be stay away from this.

May be if you say these same strategies to some of the friends who have more financial wisdom than you then there is more probability that they may appreciate you. The fact is that everyone is correct in their own way you desire more wealth it doesn't mean that the person who is next to you also have the same desire but you must keep in mind that money can solve your maximum problems and it only solves the problems related to money nothing more nothing less. You can survey in your locality you may find less or more persons who have worked hard throughout their life and at the end of their life that is in old age they don't have money to survive because they have learn the skill to make money but they never learned the skill of making money when they sleep that's the mindset which differentiate most of the common man from wealthy persons In today's world it's very easy to lose money because in ancient times we used to have coins so if want to spend you must go to market and give it physically but now we have upgraded version of spending and earning with only one click you can spend your whole money in shopping so it's necessary that one must learn how to protect money not just earning.

*Recently we came across the news
that one guy which is around 20
years old spends all of his parents
money for buying tools and gadgets
in a 3d game don't you think it's
that simple now to lose your money
At this stage there is no alternative
to investing even if you save the
inflation eating your money.
This is not rich people vs. poor
people. There are many poor people
with a rich mindset, financially poor
due to circumstance. And there are
many trust fund babies with a poor
mindset.
Rich mindset understands that the
first goal is to gain a surplus of
resources. Then, to use that surplus to*

accelerate things. Accelerate
education. Accelerate a business.
Accelerate the next generation.
Poor mindset immediately sees a
surplus as an opportunity for
consumption.
Rich mindset seeks to spend their
time, resources, and energy on work
that continues to pay off long after the
effort has been invested. Rich mindset
is all about getting a flywheel
spinning. Building momentum.
Creating systems that continue to
generate value on their own.
Poor mindset is all about the short-
term returns. Hours-for-dollars.
Resources invested without an

*immediate return are resources
wasted.*

*Rich mindset is willing to invest
resources with seemingly no reward
right away.*

*Poor mindset's immediate thought is,
"What's in it for me?" "Why pay
money to fly to that conference, pay
for the hotel, and spend all the time
when they're not even paying you?"*

*Rich mindset seeks to build
relationships based on trust, liking,
shared values, and mutual respect.*

*People with the rich mindset help
others and cultivate relationships with
no expectation of anything in return.*

*Poor mindset thinks "I scratch your
back, you scratch mine".*

Rich mindset understands that its reputation is everything, that trust and respect is earned slowly, through hard-fought, bloody effort – and that both can be lost in an instant.

Poor mindset believes it can get away with compromising its reputation to make a quick buck.

Rich mindset knows that the world isn't fair, and deals with reality swiftly, humbly, and practically. It knows the world owes it nothing, that the universe is indifferent to its existence, that the default for life is suffering and death. All successes are improbable and should be appreciated as such.

Poor mindset is consumed by the unfairness of the world, and wastes time complaining about it. It feels the world owes it something, and waits for it to be handed out.

Rich mindset celebrates the successes of others. It embraces the competition and often befriends it.

Poor mindset feels jealousy and bitterness about the successes of others. It looks at everything as a zero-sum game.

Rich mindset understands that it can never know everything, and that something can be learned from everyone.

Poor mindset deludes itself into believing it knows everything, and

that opposing perspectives are wrong
before even hearing them.

Rich mindset understands that it
cannot do everything, and that even if
it could, it would create greater value
by focusing on its core strengths. It
knows that the right team is greater
than the sum of its parts.

Poor mindset deludes itself into
thinking that it can do everything if it
just works hard enough.

Rich mindset embraces competition,
and knows that iron sharpens iron.

Poor mindset is discouraged by
competition. It complains that
"someone already got there first," or
that, "they're obviously going to

catch up to me, I might as well quit now."

Rich mindset quits strategically. It plans to quit in advance, when it realizes the potential gains of a pursuit are either unreachable with current resources or aren't worth the pain of the work involved.

Poor mind quits in reaction to pain and short-term discomfort.

Rich mindset sticks it out when the going gets tough, provided that the pursuit is worthwhile. It understands the idea of "The Dip" – that anything worth doing will be hard. It understands that the rewards are reaped by those who push through the difficulties of a pursuit precisely because the will to push through is scarce.

Poor mindset sticks things out due to stubbornness. It places too much importance on sunk costs.

Rich mindset understands that there is no "I made it". No "done". Life is defined by challenges and learning.

Poor mindset believes that one day they'll be able to "retire" – to kick back and do nothing. That all work is simply "paying dues" on the way to a life of leisure. Ironically this is the kind of mindset that stifles the ambition and drive required to ever get to the point of having that kind of life as an option.

"A wealth mindset means spending less, making wise investments, and looking for ways to improve financial standing with minimal risk. The good news is that with a little dedication, anyone can develop this mindset"

Chapter 4

To whom you can lend your money

In today's economy, it's easy to understand how someone can find themselves in a dark place financially. On the one hand, you want to help out a loved one who's in need.

On the other hand, you've heard the stories about loans gone wrong, with friendships ruined and families torn apart. Also, you may be depleting funds that you might need yourself, says Irene S. Levine, Ph.D., psychologist, author. Even if you're

sure that the asker will pay you back,
it's hard to know if you should
proceed.

To help guide you toward making the
right decision, we asked **financial
experts** to share five key things to
consider before cracking open your
wallet.

Rule 1: Only Say Yes if You Mean It
If you feel guilt-tripped into making
the loan by the asker ("I'm
desperate!") or you question your
own hesitation ("I must be a bad
person or I wouldn't feel conflicted"),
then turn her down, says Levine.

If you do cough up the cash when you
aren't sure you want to, you risk
feeling resentful, and that can cripple

the relationship before its even time for her to repay you. Not going through with the loan doesn't make you selfish or a bad friend; the response may actually protect your bond, she adds.

Levine suggests graciously declining with a sentiment like, "I'd really like to help, but I don't have the extra money to loan right now." If you feel like you need to explain further, mention an unexpected expense you were recently hit with, such as higher health insurance premiums, or something you have to save for, like your kids' college education.

Offering to help brainstorm other sources for the loan or ways to bring

*down her debt (if that's the situation)
can be a thoughtful next move. A true
friend or relative will be willing to
accept no and then thank you for any
additional help. If she doesn't, better
that your relationship sours before
you've forked over any funds.*

*Rule 2: Lend Just What You Can
Afford to Lose*

*Your friend or family member may
check all the boxes for being
trustworthy, financially stable and
reliable, but "things can happen that
prevent them from paying you back as
originally planned," says Byron Ellis,
a Certified Financial Planner™ and
managing director at Ellis and Ellis, a*

division of United Capital Financial Advisers in The Woodlands, Texas. If your loanee does get in a bind, a best friend or family member is going to be relegated to the end of the payback line, "behind the mortgage company, the credit cards, the auto loans, etc.," says Ellis. Now, imagine your stress level and the tension that would rise between you both if you actually needed that money—and she couldn't repay you.

Bottom line: Be prepared for the worst by giving only an amount that, if never returned, wouldn't jeopardize your own savings goals, bill-paying ability or other relationships.

Rule 3: Create a Firm Repayment Timeline

Ten years ago Emily White,* 43, lent her younger sister $20,000 to buy a house near their elderly parents, without discussing a repayment date for the loan. "I loved that my sister would be there for my parents, and the idea was for her to pay me back once she got settled and found a new job, since she had moved from out of state," recalls White.

But as it turned out, White's sister appeared to have another idea in mind. "Now she's been working for years, yet she hasn't mentioned anything about payback," says White. "I had no idea we were on a 10-

*years-and-counting plan. I wouldn't
be upset, but now I'm considering
some investments and that money
would help."*

*White's mistake was thinking she and
her sister were on the same page
when it came to repayment—a
situation that could have been
avoided if she had a thought-out plan.
It might seem too businesslike, but
"set specific terms for the loan that
everybody can agree to," says Ellis.
"Discuss how much money will be
loaned, interest rates and how long
they will have to pay it back." This
way, she'll know when she needs to
come up with funds, and you'll know*

when the money will be back in your account.

By nailing down this schedule, there's also no mistaking this money as a gift, adds Ellis. The loanee also can't postpone repayment indefinitely and claim she didn't know you needed it so soon.

As Ellis mentioned above, it's also wise to charge interest and work that into your repayment schedule. Depending on the amount, loaning money can involve complicated tax rules; failing to charge interest might get you in trouble. To avoid this, you may want to charge the borrower the Applicable Federal Rate (APR) as interest.

Rule 4: Always Put the Loan in Writing

Memories fade, priorities get shifted and clashing opinions over what you originally agreed to can cause problems between friends or family, says Priyanka Prakash, a finance specialist at Fit Small Business and a former business attorney.

Another benefit to having the amount and conditions in writing: Drawing up an official loan document makes it more likely that the borrower will take the loan seriously and pay it back on time. "So if you miss a payment, this is the piece of paper that we'll look at that'll help us to decide what to do, so it moves the friendship out of the way," adds Ellis.

When registered nurse Lisa Schloeder, 49, decided to help a colleague enroll in a nursing assistant program, she wanted the $1,500 loan agreement on paper. "I saw this woman at the office every day, but I still thought it was best to put everything in writing to make sure we both understood what we were getting into," remembers Schloeder.

Her foresight paid off. "There was a check waiting for me every two weeks as we had agreed, and I felt great seeing what an amazing nursing assistant she became for our practice," she says.

You can draft a simple personal loan agreement without hiring an attorney, Prakash says. But more complex deals—for example, if they involve collateral or involve more than $10,000—may require a lawyer to be involved.

Ideally, a loan agreement should be dated and state the loan amount, due date for paying it back in full, the payment schedule and any agreed-upon late payment fee (see Rule 5) or interest. Full contact information for the loaner and borrower and both of your signatures, either handwritten or electronic, are important, says Prakash.

If loaners need help pulling a formal document together, they can opt to search online for a promissory note template, which states the promise to pay someone back and can help ensure that all the important details are covered. In most states a promissory note just needs to be signed by the borrower to be valid, but it's better if you sign, too, so that the intent of both parties is clear should you have to go to court, Prakash says.

Rule 5: Never Let the Due Date Slide

If your dinero doesn't show on time, ignoring the lateness or making excuses for not confronting the borrower would be a mistake. She might continue going along as if the due date you set is a loose guideline rather than a rule.

Make it more businesslike, so neither of you feels like you're taking advantage of the other. "I did this the last time I lent money to a friend," says john, who suggests putting details about a late penalty in your written agreement; a friend would have to pay the penalty on top of the regular payment. This tactic would hopefully save you from having to send reminders ... and regret your decision to play banker.

A five-day grace period, says john, is reasonable before hitting your friend with the fine, since things do happen.

If signs are pointing to more serious delinquency—a number of scheduled payments have been missed and numerous follow-up emails or phone calls from you are ignored—it might be a good idea to consult with an attorney. "If the borrower still doesn't pay, you can take them to court," says Prakash.

In the scenario where one lump-sum payment is being paid back after a long-term loan, it never hurts to send a reminder email a month in advance of the due date to show her that you're sticking firm to the terms. For example, "According to the agreement we signed, the loan I gave you will be due on June 15. I've attached an original copy, in case you'd like to refer to it. So glad I was able to help my cousin out."

"money is your's until it's in your pocket and it's headache when it goes into others pocket in the form of loan"

Chapter 5

3 traits of self-made billionaires

There are only about <u>2,200</u> billionaires in the world — or 0.0002% of planet's population. And <u>67%</u> of those billionaires are self-made.

The members of that self-made group generally made their money in one of a few ways: they invented a useful product (think Bill Gates with Microsoft, whose net worth is around <u>$107 billion</u>); they innovated a new way of solving a problem (think

Airbnb co-founder Brian Chesky, whose net worth is around $3.7 billion); or they are savvy investors (think Warren Buffett, worth $87.3 billion). Indeed, climbing the corporate ladder will rarely get you into the club (Tim Cook who runs nearly $1 trillion company Apple, for example, is worth around $625 million).

But beyond sharp entrepreneurial and investing chops, self-made billionaires share some traits, according to Rafael Badziag, who interviewed 21 of them (including early Uber investor Tim Draper and InfoSpace and Viome founder Naveen Jain) for his book, "The Billion

Dollar Secret." Here are three of the top things they have in common, according to Badziag.

———————————

1. They succeed no matter what the 'weather' is

Badziag says it's clear why most of the general population (he calls them "drifters") don't succeed in life: They are waiting for conditions to be perfect before they strike, and often those ideal conditions never

materialize so they don't fully pursue
their dreams.

"Self-made" billionaires, he says, are
different. Most of the billionaires
Badziag interviewed didn't come from
well-off families or ideal situations,
but they pursued their dreams no
matter the circumstances around them
— no matter the "weather outside or
inside," he says.

Take for example, one of the
billionaires Badziag interviewed: N.R.
Narayana Murthy, who co-founded IT
giant Infosys, which is valued at more
than $45 billion.

The 72-year-old, who is now worth as
estimated $2.4 billion, grew up in
India in '50s and '60s, a poor country

that he says was one of the most hostile to free enterprise at the time. As a child, his family was so poor he had to sleep on the floor because they had no furniture.

But despite having no money, Murthy was eager to learn; he would go to the public library in town (he lived outside Karnataka) and read everything he could. From what he learned, Murthy believed software was the future, so in 1981 he and some colleagues got the idea to create a software company. But they didn't have a computer, and at the time, the Indian government required a license to import one, he told Badziag. So for three years, Murthy back and forth to

*Delhi by train, 1,500 miles each way,
making at least 50 visits to pitch
officials on why he should be granted
a license. With their computer and
phone line (which he says took <u>a
year</u> to procure), Murthy and his co-
founders started Infosys and grew it
from an operation with seven
employees into a global business and
one of the leading technology
consulting companies in India.*

2. They don't do it for the money

*Most "drifters" are dying to have big
incomes but never quite achieve a
high net worth status, or if they do,*

they lose motivation when they have some good in money in bank, says Badziag. (He refers to it as "the gold digger's trap.")

However, Badziag found that the "self-made" billionaires he interviewed aren't motivated by wealth. Instead, they "have a strong sense of purpose and passion for their work," and are motivated by a desire to "to grow and learn no matter how big their bank accounts get," he says.

As Apple founder Steve Jobs once famously said, "I was worth over a million dollars when i was 23 and over $10 million when I was 24, and over $100 million when I was 25. And it wasn't that important, because I never did it for the money." Jobs said he started Apple with a simple vision of trying to create a "_computer in the hands of everyday people._" and they ended up succeeding beyond they wildest dreams.

urthy told Badziag he was driven by the belief that the only way to solve the problem of poverty was "through the creation of jobs with good incomes and that entrepreneurship was the best instrument for such a solution."

And French-Syrian businessman Mohed Altrad, who made his now _$2.7 billion_ fortune by acquiring a scaffolding company in France in 1985 and growing it into the industrial services giant <u>Altrad Group</u>, told Badziag that he doesn't view money as an objective.

"It's one of the signs of success. The success of the organization is to be sustainable, in which people are happy, in which humanity finds its foundation," Altrad said.

---

3. They are frugal

"Drifters" love spending money, according to Badziag, often going into debt to spend even more than they have. Even successful people are prone to showcasing their wealth via *cars, expensive clothes and lavish vacations.*

But the billionaires Badziag interviewed were different: They "get pleasure making money, but don't enjoy spending it," he says.

Take for example, Warren Buffett, the <u>fourth-richest person</u> in the world with a net worth of around <u>$87.3 billion</u>. Despite his massive wealth, the 88-year-old still lives in the same modest Omaha house he purchased in 1958 for <u>$31,500</u> (which is around $277,00 in today's dollars). He also keeps his breakfast budget low, only spending around <u>$3.17</u> a day at McDonald's to get one of three items: two sausage patties, a sausage, egg *and cheese or a bacon, egg and cheese.*

And Peter Hargreaves, the founder of Hargreaves Lansdown, one of the UK's largest financial services businesses, told Badziag a few years back that he was still driving an eight-year-old Toyota Prius. Hargreaves' net worth is estimated at $4.2 billion. Hargreaves also told Badziag that his children were frugal too. "[My kids] drive very modest cars; they both have a car that's seven years old. They both have quite modest flats. And if they go on holiday, they go with their mates, and they go to the back of the plane," Hargreaves said.

Of course, some billionaires adjust to their level of wealth. For example, though Bill Gates is famous for wearing a $10 watch, he recently admitted that he also indulges: "Now I take lots of vacation. My 20-year-old self is so disgusted with my current self. You know, I was sure I would never fly anything but coach and you know, now I have a plane," Gates said last month at a Village Global event.

"To say more while saying less is the secret of being simple"